FROM THE CRADLE TO THE GRAVE

KATHY M. JOHNSON

JaCol Publishing Inc.
Copyright 2020 © by JaCol Publishing Inc.
Illustrations Copyright © 2020 by JaCol Publishing Inc.
FIRST PRINTING
December 2020
All rights reserved
JaCol Publishing Inc.
195 Murica Aisle
Irvine, CA 92614
818-510-2898
Editor-in-Chief: Randall Andrews
www.jacolpublishing.com

ISBN: 978-1-946675-53-8

No part of this publication may be reproduced in whole or part, or stored in a retrieval system, or transmitted in any form, or by other means, electronic, mechanical, photocopying, recording, or otherwise without written permission of the publisher, except in the case of brief quotations embodied in critical articles and reviews. The classroom teacher may reproduce the materials in this book for use in a single classroom only.

Cover Art by Karen Edwards

To my big brother, Thayner-aka, Johnny Sitton:
You and I have been through so much together. You were my first friend, and taught me about love and loyalty. You didn't want to play paper dolls, but you did, and I wanted to play with you so I played trucks and many other "boy" games. We had real honest fun, you and I. I was a little tomboy because of you, and I would not trade the fun, laughter, and tears for anything. Thank God we didn't grow up in the electronic age. We never would have crossed the lake in mud-encrusted boats and hole-filled rafts, with a stick and a can, and a promise that this was going to be a great day. We rode motorcycles all over the country, and you always went first. Not because you requested it, but because I looked up to you and didn't trust myself until you trusted me. You would show me that it was okay, and then we could carry on about the business at hand. Namely, it was all about adventure and daring. Thank you for the times that you were kind and gentle with me. It wasn't all the time, but it was often enough to burn the memory into my heart. I love you, big brother.

To my girls, Kara and Kylie, if it were not for you two, I don't know where I would be. You have given me the strength and courage to go on, and I love each of you more than life itself.

To my editor, Randall Andrews, thank you for pushing me when I felt like giving up, and for all of the support.

To my friend and BBP, (bestest buddy pal), Judy Paulson, thank you for being a dear lifelong friend and supporter.

To my friend and BFF, Nina Fields, thank you for your undying friendship and love.

To my sis and dearest friend, Connie Rudd, thank you for liking all of my poems, and for being a great friend.

To My dear friend, George Tveden, thank you for your love, support, and friendship.

Last but far from least, to my sissy, Kamie Norling, thank you for typing the book for me, and for your constant support and love.

Contents

1. 1st poem, written at 7-years-old. — 1
2. To Hold — 2
3. Insomnia — 4
4. Storm — 6
5. Resurrected — 7
6. Undercurrent — 8
7. No Recall — 9
8. Dusk — 10
9. Want — 12
10. Gone — 13
11. Kup — 14
12. War — 16
13. Tough Row to Hoe — 17
14. Mind Play — 19
15. I can't — 21
16. Blackness — 23
17. Convalescent Home — 24
18. Unscathed — 26
19. Collapse — 28
20. Numma — 29
21. The Cabin — 31
22. Introductions — 33
23. Death Follows Birth — 34
24. To My Grandfather — 36
25. Firstborn Grandchild — 38
26. Regrets — 40
27. Huntress — 43
28. Arizona Musings II — 45
29. If My Life Was a Story — 46
30. Autumn — 49
31. Deceit — 50
32. Homeless Holiday — 52
33. Clarity — 54

34. PTSD	57
35. The Worth of Me	59
36. The Guest	60
37. Without You	61
38. The Dingy	63
39. For My Niece, Christy	65
40. Lost to Monday	66
41. Yard Sale	68
42. For My Aunt Yvonne	70
43. Mirror	72
44. Heartache	74
45. Birthday	76
46. Death	77
47. So Sublime	79
48. Lonely	80
49. The Winner	82
50. Musings in Arizona 1	84
51. Uncle Timothy Ryan McDonough	86
52. Final Curtain	88
53. Absence of Color	90
About the Author	93

1st poem, written at 7-years-old.

The leaves are falling,
    They are red, green, and brown.
    I like to play in them and roll on the ground,
    But it soon will be winter
    And leaves blow away,
    Then when it snows,
    We'll find new games to play.

2

To Hold

I hold you,
    Waiting
    For your last breath.

Your breathing changes
    And I stay,
    Momentarily forgetting
    That you will
    Soon be gone.

Nothing
    To hold onto.
    Nothing
    To let go of.

Holding you,

From the Cradle to the Grave

I hear your last breath.

You died.
    I lived,
    Wanting you
    To hold me.

Insomnia

A candle burns at both ends
    Daylight to dark
    Unforgiving
    A restless soul.

Shut your eyes
    Hearing the beating
    The endless relentlessness
    Hovers
    With all that is unforgotten.

Your gift of nocturnal hours
    Cries out for resolution
    Short-circuiting thoughts
    Where is the off mode?

. . .

From the Cradle to the Grave

Work begins
    I am left alone
    Hearing the beating
    Of your heart
    A candle burns at both ends.

4

Storm

The wind is hollow grey
    Hard rain continues.
    Earth is a muddy victim 'til summer.
    I pray the weather foregoes the innocence.
    I hear the thunder, and see the lightning
    In this virgin forest.
    Simple plans become cumbersome
    In this relentless downpour.
    Shy and unyielding, answers come.
    It is advised not to question
    The conquered nature
    Of the beast.

5

Resurrected

Gentle moments pass by.
    Suffocate this space
    I dreamt I still held.
    Once, a child wild and free.
    Promises held,
    Like a moth to a flame.
    Collapse in charcoal embers
    Of yesterday once more.
    I flee this place-
    Unburied as a corpse resurrected.
    Dying to live,
    Or living to die.
    I awaken my soul
    To encompass tender moments.
    Lost, and alone,
    I reach for someone not there.
    Tears fall,
    Like memories die,
    To an untrained eye.

6

Undercurrent

People pace to drone together,
    Gather here, a public place.
    Robed in black and scarlet streaming,
    River rocks diffuse the face.
    Psuedo-feet, they crowd much closer,
    Hover near the currents edge.
    Tragic angels eyes all gleaming,
    Rescue crews onlookers bled.
    Swollen blue, then drag the shoreline-
    A cadaver hook will never tire.
    Caught flesh is bait for hungry viewers-
    Buzzing voices reel stale air.
    Robed in white, with haloes rising,
    Gaping mouths all fat and fed.
    Lines later buzz with conversation-
    Halos fall and robes are shed.

No Recall

I am left here, afraid.
    I tried to hide,
    But you were there,
    Taking my soul away.
    I don't remember when it began.
    I don't remember how it ended.
    When I returned,
    Blackness and fear surrounded me.
    I am lost for what to say
    To the faces that stare back at me.
    So strange,
    What brought on these nightmares?
    I wonder if it matters?
    When I am dead, I might be free.
    How do I stop awakening to two worlds?
    One is quiet and dark,
    And you are in the other.

8

Dusk

I walk this path alone,
    Seek answers untold.
    No guarantees or refunds
    In this mindless Hell.

I stand forthright and determined,
    Endlessly somber and calculated,
    For answers found here
    In life's moments unfair.

I sit with my regrets-
    Digging into my soul,
    Cold and unfeeling.
    Call out to no one.

It is the dusk of life
    And memories fail me.

From the Cradle to the Grave

I reach for an answer
To questions unasked.

I know the drill here.
    Regurgitate the words back.
    Lose all control of my direction,
    As I run for the shelter…

Mindless enemies come close,
    Challenge me to a dual.
    I accept, indignant and fierce,
    With fear written on my face.

I rely on my burdens,
    To take me away.
    Misfortune shines bright,
    And I take the query to task.

I question the sunset
    As it dims and falls.
    I question the dusk,
    Afraid of the dark.

9

Want

I walk on stone
    Hard and cold.
    Waves cover
    As the light
    Of the moon
    Washes
    Diamonds
    All around.
    I reach
    As it runs
    Through
    My fingers.
    Sacred,
    I bow.
    Restless
    Like an addict,
    I scream.
    Muffled by the roar.
    Oh the want
    Of wanting more.

10

Gone

You, moments from gone.
    Can't shake this off.
    Who are you?
    What remains,
    Just the last line,
    On a piece of stained paper.
    A living will,
    Coffee cups all around.
    I toss other documents
    Into a filling trash bin.
    When did you put all this away?
    More words on a page,
    Trying to keep you alive.
    I have to go home,
    Knowing I have work to do,
    To care for you.

11

Kup

In the twilight, I look for you.
    I seek warmth
    And a chance
    For a glimpse of undying love.
    The winter wind blows cold.
    No songbirds can be heard singing.
    They huddle together
    In a shared warmth.
    I know, tomorrow,
    The sky will be over cast.
    The chill will remain.

I want to follow you,
    Chase away the darkness,
    And overcome hate with love.

I miss you.
    I want to hold you,

From the Cradle to the Grave

By the fires glow.
I roll the claddagh ring
On my finger,
A gift from you-
A glimps of friendship,
Love, and loyalty.

I reach out for tomorrow.
    Yesterday creeps back.
    There's no return from here.
    I still love you.

12

War

Life
    So callously
    Sent.
    Given
    To an endless
    Fight
    Of hate and fear.
    Left to
    Foreign soil
    In tears of blood.

13

Tough Row to Hoe

The last tear fell
    Before anger took hold.
    I saw her smile,
    Bitterness to behold.

Drops of hatred splash
    In my face-aged.
    I lift my head,
    Cleanse with sage.

Smoke clouded room,
    Where bad will flee.
    I ache to hold you,
    Set ourselves free.

You are the winner,
    For I am so lost.

KATHY M. JOHNSON

>There is no forgiveness.
>Joy is the cost.

>I run to the edge.
>>Peace set me free.
>>I am so sorry
>>If you would let me be.

>Dark edges crowd me.
>>Nowhere to decline.
>>Reach out in prayer,
>>Will you be mine?

>I held that hand so long ago,
>>Rocked you while you slept.
>>I could never let go,
>>Though I felt so inept.

>Is it the final tear?
>>So glad I don't know.
>>It's a long walk out
>>And a tough row to hoe.

14

Mind Play

I reach out toward nothing,
    Call wild in the wind.
    My soul aches for closure.
    You play solitaire
    As if a command performance,
    Prohibitive to a melancholy day.
    Rain falls, relentless,
    Washes away tears
    Evident to a rabid observer.
    No casual encounter.
    Abides here and now,
    Just intense banter.
    Sought to hide in vain,
    You recognize the scent,
    As sweet wood smolders.
    I take the extinguisher,
    Cold and damp,
    Not unlike our love.
    Identify this song,

KATHY M. JOHNSON

With the words all wrong.
Callous as mechanics hands,
I bow out.
Save the last dance for me.

15

I can't

Something comes through.
    I find no answers here.
    I look through the window,
    See the dim setting
    Of the evening sun.
    I can't see you.
    I feel the soft blanket
    Made especially for me.
    I taste the black tea,
    My favorite drink.
    I smell the vanilla candle,
    Go into a trance.
    As it's light glows.
    I can't hold you.
    I walk to the street,
    Where shoes and gravel meet.
    I can't see your light.
    Set off the motion detector.
    I can't feel you.

KATHY M. JOHNSON

Shadows fade.
You are not here to cast one.
I am alone
With the beating of my heart.

16

Blackness

Reveal to me
    What makes you
    Tick.
    Energy endless
    Cries out
    For reform.
    Truth belittled,
    I stumble,
    Unseen,
    Like a thief
    In the night.
    It darkens.
    I call to you,
    With broken voice,
    Second hand
    Sweeps.
    Batteries not included.

17

Convalescent Home

"Would you like a snip of wine?"
    She asked.
    I said, "not today, Numma."
    "I don't think I have wine anyway." she laughed.
    She offered my grands candy,
    And questioned if they would like
    To pet her kitten.
    It was nowhere to be found,
    And we all giggled.
    Numma used to boat
    With my mom,
    Daughters,
    And me.
    Such a loving, wonderful lady,
    And friend.
    Watch thoughts waver,
    As she tilted her head,
    And smiled.
    Sadness seeped in.
    She is going away.

Memories appear and disappear
In a blink.
We grinned at each other,
And I wonder if it's my mind
Escaping me.
"No. It Alzheimer's," the caregiver said.

Unscathed

My heart withers unspoken.
    Beats silent from old pain.
    Hopes never dreamt of pass by
    As the tears flow in vain.

Obscure and forbidden thoughts
    Carved initials in bone.
    Trees left unscathed stand solid
    Left to answer no one.

Am I distraught from absence?
    Or is it as it seems?
    Another lone night drives by-
    Lights muster shattered screams.

Is this love forsaken now?
    I hold you in my mind.

Yet from the stars shed nothing.
This ache inside unkind.

Are you a crazed monster
    Cold, damp, and unaware?
    Should I reach my hand out once
    To simply say I care?

Broken are the older dreams
    Cuts too deep to heal now.
    My new thoughts are all of you,
    Daunted love I must show.

You are lost to many here.
    Eye contact is still stares.
    I want to reach you once more.
    It's all my heart will bear.

My heart withers unspoken,
    Beats silent from old pain.
    Hopes never dreamt of pass by,
    As the tears flow in vain.

19

Collapse

No rounding of the edges-
    So stark, blatant. and real.
    Words not pressured
    To produce a diamond.
    No fossil fuels to create.
    I see your eyes lit up
    Above a stalling mouth.
    Your words collapse
    As the living do for death.
    No further spoken sound.
    Hunger releases the gasps.
    Not dead, but no longer living.

20

Numma

Old hands pressed to an aging face.
    Years of work and sunshine scars
    Take back the glow of youth.
    Energy waning in musty air.
    Antique fears and wayward tears
    Roll salty and stings her eyes.
    She bites her lip-longs for days gone by.
    Incessant cries as a wolf in hunger.
    She sits in her chair beguiled.
    Alzheimers steals the new day and past.
    A smile appears as I sit beside her and hold her hand.
    Thin skin and vivid veins scream winter years.
    She was at her best in the other seasons of life,
    But waiting on the hilltop the view has changed.
    She held the kitten no one else sees,
    Pets her sweater as gently as can be.
    She was my moms best friend for many years,
    But mom left too soon,
    Yet I wonder. would it be as difficult,
    To see her stare out the window

KATHY M. JOHNSON

With nothing in mind but who sits here this day.
Loss is so contrived and what constitutes it.
My tears begin to fall, lonely and alone,
As would a dehydrated dream.
The days of early boating always stay.
She grasps my hand holding this moment.
Is there room for fear in your brave mind?
Or is it just holding on to a piece of yesterday?
I miss you.

21

The Cabin

Green light through the shade
    Shown onto the pebbled road.
    That rough stump of wood
    Cracked and peeled
    Like dad's hands.
    Not delicate but worn
    like the Giving Tree.
    Generous and stately,
    brought tears to my eyes.
    The river wrapped around,
    a serpent ready to strike.
    I miss the old boat,
    skimming through rapids.
    In the Snake River Canyon.
    A dream fulfilled a thousand times.
    The Blue Mountains
    Heavy with snow.
    A skiers paradise.
    The light grew dim,
    So I limped back to the cabin.

KATHY M. JOHNSON

A horse needing shot.
I met him at the door,
More weathered than I,
With a glisten in his eyes.
Fire burning low-
I am once again thankful.

22

Introductions

Hovering yellow and red
    Introduce the day's sunset.
    Glimpses of shadows
    Disappear as the glow subsides..
    Darkness is tonight's guest.
    Shade, in spite of absent trees-
    Night sky is clear and cold.
    Each breath forms a fog.
    Blessings, present but not stated.
    Thankfulness fills my soul.
    I ponder in the lingering dark,
    Given that light will come
    While early morning dew
    Introduces the day's sunlight.

23

Death Follows Birth

The moment of birth
   Marks the disease
   On my doorstep
   Death flutters and flaunts.
   I wish it away
   But it hovers full flame.
   Death controls us from birth
   I push death away
   It mocks my attempts
   On my doorstep
   It flutters and flaunts.
   The moment of birth
   Marks the disease
   We're born dying
   As death circles birth
   And dares me to hide.
   For a moment or two
   We gain a reprieve
   But not to wonder
   If we're free.

From the Cradle to the Grave

Just moments for a fool
Death dances with me
The moment of birth
Marks the disease
On my doorstep
Death flutters and Flaunts.

24

To My Grandfather

You taught me to have patience
    Enough to search beyond shamrocks
    To four leaf clovers.
    You told me I shouldn't walk
    Under ladders or in front
    Of black cats.
    You saw me cheat at solitaire,
    Told me I was cheating myself
    Then set up new rules
    For me to follow:
    Three tries to win-
    If you haven't, put the cards
    Away for awhile.
    You found thirteen four leaf clovers
    One day,
    And gave
    All of them to me.
    You told me you had a fifty-fifty
    Chance to live or die.
    I didn't know what cancer meant

From the Cradle to the Grave

But you squeezed my hand,
Gave me a nickel for a coke,
Said to look both ways
Before I crossed
The road, and your eyes
Told me cancer was bad.
You were in Kootenai Hospital
For surgery,
They said I was too young,
To come in,
But you let me sneak
Around to your window
So we could make
Each other feel better.
They said you wouldn't get out
But I knew you would
And you were home
For Christmas and New Year's
And until January 27th.
The snow was too deep
For clover but I played
Solitaire three times,
All day long.
Then people came in with food
And a man sat in your chair.
Family and friends cried
Off and on, all day,
But I knew Spring was soon
And then life begins, so I waited.
The clovers were alongside
The house
Where you told me they grew best.
I picked three for you,
And didn't look for more.

25

Firstborn Grandchild

He is a handsome lad
    All of eleven years old.
    He handles the bass
    As if polishing gold.

I recall his small hand
    Enclosed in mine
    I felt like a million
    And never had a dime.

I walked with him
    Held him on my knee
    But now he's fast
    And waits for me.

He is kind, sweet, and loving
    His laugh melts my heart.

From the Cradle to the Grave

A photo of his smile
Comforts me when we part.

He talks about when he grows up
    And what happens when I die
    I let him know I love him
    How I felt when my grandma died.

I will never truly leave him.
    His guardian angel I will be
    And if he feels alone
    The rain or shine will be me.

26

Regrets

I peek through the curtain
    As my past marches by.
    Sadly, I recognize it
    And I begin to cry.

Shortcomings all too many
    Mistakes hover like crows
    My faults rise to the surface.
    How am I to grow?

The "I love you "I forgot to say
    The "I'm sorry" I didn't tell
    Make me wish for a redo
    To spare me from this hell.

I thought that I remembered you,
    I thought I felt things right,

From the Cradle to the Grave

But the skeletons in the closet
Pour over me with fright.

I know I should have done better,
    And certainly should have done more.
    I know because this morning
    You slammed the final door.

My eyes sting from the tears,
    My lips hurt from the bite.
    Can you please forgive me-
    allow me to see some light?

It's dark and cold this morning
    I stumble to a walk.
    I can't do this without you-
    Can you release these locks?

Mind prison is a horrific place.
    I want to once again be free.
    Please remove these shackles
    Allow me to escape and be.

The lights are on as usual.
    I walk with no place to go.
    I wish to join the party,
    And not feel sad and low.

I made so many mistakes
    And reach out for your hand.

KATHY M. JOHNSON

    You are cold and bitter.
    My losses flow like sand.

I say I'm sorry once,
    Then say it ten more times.
    You never answer me
    I am left quite blind.

Forgiveness is a blessing
    Bestowed upon a few.
    I will be here waiting,
    And I do forgive you.

27

Huntress

The fish said to my hook
    "Would you please pardon me?"
    I am living in this brook
    Just like I want to be.

I stood a bit astonished
    Why would the fish speak free?
    I had a hook prepared
    But my fish he could not be.

I thought about the wildlife
    What else seeks home beneath.
    I shot a deer the year before
    And her yearling I did meet.

I closed my eyes to think a bit
    I've always loved nature here

But could I fit in
If I relate to it by fear?
I took my hook and put it away
A mushroom I did eat.
It was not very filling
But was indeed a treat.

I quit watching Bambi
   Since many tears did fall
   I choked up on the creatures
   And loved them one and all.

But what about my family
   Fish and meat they need
   I'll call the local grocer
   to see if he has my steed.

I wandered in the moonlight
   Then sat in the sun.
   I wanted to find the answer
   Before no longer young.

Fish and meat are not the same
   The grocer admitted it was so.
   So I stepped out into the wild
   Asked how can I live without a bow?

The elk he looked quite haggard
   And I his friend would be
   But watch out for the family
   And all who have a gate key.

28

Arizona Musings II

In the midst of air streams,
    I feel the sun embrace my soul.
    Invisible, I gather stones,
    For the night cool will come.
    I laugh for a moment.
    Then the moments gone.
    Etched in lines grown old
    I savored the peace within.
    Palm trees wave hello or goodbye,
    For who would know the difference?
    Entrapped, I reach out my hand,
    To embrace the solemn thunder.
    Clouds drift, ebb and flow.
    I am left with my heartbeat.
    Who would know the joy,
    Echoed back, familiar and refined.
    This is life lived in conquest,
    As the sun beats a different rhythm
    Light shines bright, brings chills
    And I am as one with all the world.

29

If My Life Was a Story

If my life was a story
    And my thoughts free to tell
    Maybe you could understand
    Why life is like Hell.

Try to remain strong
    Take life in stride
    It always turns out wrong
    That is why thoughts hide.

Keeping problems in
    Not letting people know
    It's rough to begin
    So again problems grow.

Everyone has trouble

From the Cradle to the Grave

Why add mine too
Yours would be double
It's a thing I can't do.

It isn't one thing
    Rather additions to each day
    living a chaotic life
    Trying to find a way.

Go through life
    Yet wonder, why?
    Fighting and strife
    A world of lies.

Run here, run there,
    Pass life's cause
    No one really cares
    Never stop or pause.

Another day nears
    existence carries on
    Does anyone hear?
    Life is all gone.

Wish I could say
    What disrupts my mind
    It would take all day
    There isn't the time.

. . .

KATHY M. JOHNSON

If my life was a story
    And my thoughts free to tell
    Maybe you could understand
    Why life is like Hell.

30

Autumn

You approach the steam iron,
    Back arched like a rainbow.
    I could have names you Bootsie:
    Tan feet splashed onto charcoal fur.
    The iron spits as you ballet closer.
    A diamond pupil draws out the green of your eyes.
    The hair on your tail
    Fans out like porcupine quills.
    I could call you Morris,
    But your finicky act is shorter
    Than the electric can opener.
    I unplug the iron
    And dish up a bowl of nine lives.
    Your body snarls disapproval,
    At the irons whispered hiss of steam.
    You hook the hot metal,
    Then echo backward,
    Settling for savory stew.

31

Deceit

The hand curls around my neck,
    Time to play this game.
    It is dark and cold out here
    And I don't know your name.

I run up to the waters edge.
    I gently washed my feet.
    I held on for dear life
    In case we dare not speak.

"What do you want today?"
    Said the spider to the fly,
    "I want a piece of you
    I want to feel you die."

I offered up a piece of bread,
    The body of all life.

From the Cradle to the Grave

Had no wine to offer
The blood will come with strife.

Colors gathered 'round me.
    Red stood out the most.
    Is this the final offering?
    Lest I should boast.

Stars and stripes burst in the air.
    The finale gathered 'round.
    Who am I to stop this fun?
    As webs weave o'er the ground.

The carcass washes outward.
    Was it ever here?
    Absence makes the heart grow fond,
    And even brings a tear.

The cool around my ankles,
    The cool around my neck.
    This trap is set lightly,
    I may be coming back.

32

Homeless Holiday

In the dim of the night
 I hear them respond
 to the anguished calls
 And thunderous roar.

It is the season of giving,
 But not all receive
 The gifts of life,
 And the rewards unending.

Love is rampant here,
 Yet he is all alone.
 Tents on the riverbank
 For this holiday home.

Hunger abounds
 Mouths left unfed.

From the Cradle to the Grave

The chill of the air
Is tonight's blanket.

Eyes never meet now.
    Hollow promises untold-
    Cold chills wrap their bodies.
    It is so inhumane.

Lights flicker on the trees,
    Reflect on his glazed eyes.
    Somber liquid falls
    On the forgotten hearts.

33

Clarity

I just woke up
    I'm still not here
    I feel just like
    I've had a beer.

Am I awake?
    Am I alone?
    I hear a ring-
    Is that my phone?

You waltz by
    Upon a cloud.
    The Angels wait
    In a big old crowd.

What's going on?
    Is their a doubt

From the Cradle to the Grave

What went on
While I was out?

The sheet is crumpled
    I'm in a sweat
    The windows open
    Have we met?

I grasp the phone
    Oh, it's you.
    Can you come over?
    I think it's flu.

I shook my head,
    Stretched my toes.
    A tear rolled down
    Dripped off my nose.

I'm not in fear,
    Thou blurry I be.
    I can't stand up
    And unclearly I see.

My friend walked in
    Said, "coffees on."
    What a relief
    The ring is gone.

I have a cup
    Then two or three.

KATHY M. JOHNSON

    I'm waking up,
    Worried I be.

I see things clear
    The Angel laughed.
    You set the stage
    And I have not passed.

Not actually hearing
    But pretending quite well
    I stood for a moment
    And in bed I fell.

34

PTSD

Wait in the timid air,
    Shy as an unridden horse.
    Spasms erupted from every muscle
    No shame in anxiety,
    Poured out into heavy chains.
    Burden the present with the past.
    Screams come from inside him-
    Lost soul rejected after service.
    Sit on cracked pallets
    Quivers offered up pain not deserved-
    Yet wanted, to stop this emotion ridden life.
    Who would stand by
    To strip honor from this empty man?
    Cries ring out into the streets,
    Only his echo returns.
    Tremble yourself to sleep-
    Nightmares bring horrific memories
    To the surface, you are awake.
    Nowhere to go.
    Records only show, "Soldier, homeless,

Mentally disturbed;" Not a hero's welcome.
Blood flooded in a horrible gun fire flashback.
Eyes open, only to the pounding of his heart.
Cold fear runs rampant
Day; Streets begin to fill.
Nowhere to go-
Nowhere to hide.
Hallucinations come in flashes of truth.
"Where is home?", he asked himself softly
It escaped rigid and unfeeling.
"So this is my country."

35

The Worth of Me

I have offered you
    My hand in friendship.
    I will be there
    When you need me,
    And will always answer
    Your early or late night calls.
    My word means more
    Than golden promises
    And pinky swears.
    I will stand by them,
    For the worth of my words
    Is the worth of me.
    No need to take
    With a grain of salt.
    I mean it-
    Straight up.

36

The Guest

Sun shines through the trees,
    As the lake glares back.
    Smooth reflections hide
    Time into sunset autumn.
    Colors leap from the tamarack-
    Bid farewell to this day.
    Short and ill-tempered,
    The west winds blow,
    Hover in this valley
    Stabilized by bull pines
    With needles swept away
    Like a long lost friend
    Engaged in dance,
    Alone on a still night-
    Bids farewell to an unknown guest
    Hidden from sight.

37

Without You

I'm glad that you were born
  Even though you are not here.
  I don't want to be alone,
  And it's my constant fear.

You ran out of my life,
  Which set my world on fire
  I am praying for rain-
  My heart has grown so tired.

You say I did you wrong
  And play a victims role
  You say you disown me,
  And it's out of my control.

I catch a glimpse of you
  Every now and then.

KATHY M. JOHNSON

    I want to hold you tight
    Like I did back when.

My soul aches so badly,
    I miss your funny ways.
    My head is full of clouds,
    And I am in a daze.

I don't know how to say goodbye,
    I never was that good.
    But I will be here waiting
    Just in case I should.

38

The Dingy

Mountain air echos
    Elevating the tale
    Ocean tides call me
    A beckon to sail
    Empty boats call out
    Peaceful and still
    Alone in the quiet
    No void to be filled
    Joining the waters
    So cold and calm-
    I reach to the sky
    All is quiet, solemn
    The thinker silent
    The mourner is lost
    The baby bust stares
    Any effort will cost
    In wonder and fear
    Leaving alone now
    Hating the mirror
    The crowd is so quiet

KATHY M. JOHNSON

Numbed to the pain
Now I'll be going
Appears the same
I heard my heart beating
Questions unknown
I'm leaving this place
Aged yet not grown.

39

For My Niece, Christy

She was a bright light.
    To hear her laugh
    Brightened dark days.
    A mother like no other,
    She nurtured her boys-
    Loved without question,
    Unconditionally.
    She fixed my hair and makeup
    For special occasions.
    She had a heart of pure gold.
    I will miss your smile.
    I will miss your bold way
    Of standing against wrong.
    I love you
    And will miss you.
    You are a bright light.

40

Lost to Monday

The sunrise and alarm
    Clocks failed to win
    When we closed
    The world down
    For that day
    Nothing else mattered
    When we cooled a bottle
    Of wine and forgot
    To break the seal
    And it became warm
    From the broken lights
    Through the shades
    We would hide from the sun
    Retreating below
    The routine we liked to break
    Once again broken
    You whispered
    That our morning
    Had continued into night

From the Cradle to the Grave

Holding on to you and Monday
Once more.

41

Yard Sale

Little troll
    With long green hair.
    I saw you
    Peak out from a pile.
    Childhood memories
    Flow in soft, dry air.
    You gave me good fortune,
    A lucky hand
    To draw from.
    I loved you
    But you disappeared
    Like a cat in the dark
    Life turned the corner,
    Briefly I sought you.
    The Lord said,
    "Put all your faith in me
    Trust my grace
    No idols before me."
    You died for my sins,

From the Cradle to the Grave

Whole by your stripes.
Good bye my little charm.

42

For My Aunt Yvonne

God, sometimes I wonder
    At the second chances you give-
    But there's an Aunt I love so much
    And I want you to let live.

She's neither youth nor old,
    But the precious in between.
    She is beyond my ignorance
    And her offering should be seen.

"Why does the sun set grandma?"
    "Friend what should I do now?"
    "Mom, will you please pick up the phone?"
    But Lord she needs you now.

She hasn't always followed your ways,
    But a sinner she is not.

From the Cradle to the Grave

She helps most of your children,
Her intention's the best you've got.

I ask you, oh so humbly,
    I always have believed.
    If you get to know her better
    You'll see she must not leave.

She's with all of your children
    All who ask receive.
    God she needs your help now
    Her side you must not leave.

43

Mirror

It lies to me,
    Says I am old
    I can't perfect
    Crows feet gone bold.

My hands wrinkle,
    Like my face, blind
    Age crept quickly,
    Like thieves unkind.
    The child inside
    Screams out, I'm young.
    These bones crackle
    Speaks from the tongue.

Jump off place nears
    I view my hands,
    No longer smooth
    I see a glance.

From the Cradle to the Grave

. . .

Age defies me,
>   Oh, yesterday.
>   It's all so clear
>   The cruel ways.

Hair turns silver,
>   Gravity wins,
>   As eyes droop tired
>   I sit again.

From the cradle
>   To the graveyard,
>   It came so soon,
>   I bow my head.

Reflections here
>   Show the outside.
>   Inner beauty
>   Seldom abides.

Youth remembered,
>   Turns oh so bright,
>   Echos back past
>   Turn out the light.

My head is strong,
>   My heart heavy,
>   Darkness enters-
>   Steals all glory.

44

Heartache

A hole, alone and colored black
    Surmises to play games with my mind.
    I add people to my life,
    But they don't fill this hollow place.
    The moon set low tonight
    A dim light to follow.
    I seek to find the secret of despair.
    It is cold and unfulfilled here.
    As I look for a warm space,
    The spring snow sabotages my hope.
    Experience cool, dampness
    Sought out of days and people now gone.
    Sunshine appears, yet I am in the shade.
    It likes to escape me.
    This search for comfort defies efforts.
    I help my heart gently in search of relief.
    The agony on the surface now gone.
    A hole, lonely and colored black.
    Since you left my heart has a hole,

From the Cradle to the Grave

No one else can fill, so I mourn.
You are not returning from death.
Death is cold and unfulfilled.
I knew that the day I lost you.

Birthday

Lines
    Shown on her face.
    Years of sun
    Worship
    Etched a memory
    Into the furrowed brow.
    Laugh lines unkind-
    Eyes penetrate
    At a glance.
    The count begins.
    Never a winner
    Anymore.

46

Death

Death is a reminder
    Our stay here is short.
    Death is an opportunistic
    Seeker of body and mind.
    On his last leg-
    One foot in the grave,
    Looks like death
    Appears to be dying
    Slow but steady decline.
    He sought the reaper-
    Dirty, down, and ugly.
    Life's blood poured
    Freely, without regard.
    For the man's heart
    Or woman's lungs-
    It drifts in, a stranger
    In the night.
    Taking all in his path.
    Fragile fire stripping
    All in its way.

KATHY M. JOHNSON

Opportunity knocks.
Live life, for one day
Again, before the end,
Death Knocked-
No one answered the door
Laugh death in the face...
It's not worthy of perspective,
But it will take us all
At some critical point.
Death is the taker.
Birth is the giver-
We are all dying.

47

So Sublime

I reach out for your warm body-
    A pillow is all I find.
    I am caught lonely without you
    No reason or rhyme.
    Your eyes saw right through me.
    Your lips like a puzzle fit mine.
    Your touch is like no other,
    I did have the time of my life.
    Now you've left me here to abide
    Everyday niceties and life not sublime.
    If I could hold you one more time
    Don't know what my favorite part would be
    I'd focus on your blue eyes,
    And live to the moment before it ended.

48

Lonely

Nothing comes by
    Find no answers here
    Air rushes through
    The open window view
    I can't see you.
    The sun setting,
    Yellow and orange,
    Smell of barbecue
    Smoke and sauce
    It is fresh in my window
    I can't smell you.
    Rough wood needs sanded,
    Filed, hawthorne tree
    Flattened my tire,
    I can't feel you.
    The candle light puts
    Me in a trance.
    I see my shadow
    Walk to the street
    Where cement and gravel

From the Cradle to the Grave

Meet,
Set off the emotion
Detector, it's still
Just you and me
I guess I'm lonely-
Not alone.

49

The Winner

I stand against time
    Linger with untold tales.
    This day has begun
    Unafraid and emboldened
    I wait.
    Yesterday in the distance
    Calls upon today.
    A warm invitation
    To stand for something,
    For anything.
    The west wind blows
    Beckons this child
    To choose wisely.
    Up from down
    Or right from wrong.
    There is no prize
    For second place.
    Complacency becomes a sin
    Valid and weak.
    Pitted against one another

From the Cradle to the Grave

We fight
For the right to matter.
In the distance,
Tomorrow waits
An uninvited guest,
Mocks my decision
To play dead.

50

Musings in Arizona I

The call to truth
    Comes easily
    For mouths that close
    More dormant still.

Words flow outright
    Flecks in the night
    For the righteous
    Who shall not touch.

But who yells forth,
    Angry, bitter?
    To take the stage
    This one act show.

I call out,
    I am not dead.

From the Cradle to the Grave

Silence echoes back
But who would hear?

In the cold, damp,
    Words become dice.
    Trickery, yes,
    Deceives our eyes.

Half that you see,
    And half that you hear
    Are fallacy-
Dead drums at night.

I see the moon
    Glimmered delights.
    Then the sun rises
    Erodes all traces.

Did it exist?
    Was it for real?
    Or a figment
    Imagined once?

Uncle Timothy Ryan McDonough

We traveled to Wyoming,
    Which on my part was a whim.
    I wanted to see a new state,
    And decided "I'll go with him."
    We had many adventures,
    And lots of good times-
    When you applied for jobs,
    I did too for it was no crime.

When Daniels called me
    And hadn't called you,
    I was in shock,
    Didn't know what to do.

The first day of work,
    I arrived dressed in heels.
    They handed me a shovel to dig mud-
    I thought, "what's the deal?"

. . .

But you found a job,
    Just down the hill-
      We had great visits,
      Told jokes I think of still.

When you passed in 2008,
    I thought of all the fun
    And how I figured,
    It had only just begun.

You were my friend,
    And my uncle too.
    I miss you when it's summer,
    Sun high and the skys so blue.

I wish you were here today-
    To celebrate life.
    I'll toast to you,
    And smile, not cry.

Hold my moms hand,
    Enjoy your special world.
    I'm happy you have each other,
    In the light of the Lord.

52

Final Curtain

In the still moments of night,
    I ponder the rights and wrongs
    Of this world.
    I lay down my guard-
    Anticipate future chaos and ills.
    This place feels dark and cold,
    Winter's midnight in feelings.
    The guard appears to sleep
    Unencumbered by this terror.
    Hatred abounds-
    The good seem to be lost,
    Looking for a light of truth.
    Looking for a shade of grey.
    It's not all black and white.
    But extremes take control.
    The classroom is empty-
    Make way for idle minds
    Filled with distant hindsight.
    Evil dances on the headstones
    Of those lost and the unfound.

From the Cradle to the Grave

I hide,
Unable to make a decision.
Hatred abounds,
As shadows
Grow.
There is no free admission-
Just echoes of my anguished call.
Joy becomes a distant memory
As pain surfaces in overdrive.
There is no answer here-
Just questions, stale and mocked.
Truth becomes the enemy
And blends as ill-fated illusion.
The final curtain falls
And life is the price of admission.
Confusion abounds
And love is all I have.
It may be enough.

53

Absence of Color

He walks down distant streets
    Alone, he marks the day
    Cold and unfeeling feet
    Greet him on the path.
    Evil
    For its own sake
    Ebbs and flows
    As color becomes key.
    Strikes out against him,
    Blood red as mine.
    He can't fight back.
    Who would believe him?
    Beaten and bruised
    Day turns to dusk.
    Flesh torn and tattered–
    Who would defend him?
    Not here,
    Not on this day.
    Authoritarian men laugh
    For it's not theirs to worry.

From the Cradle to the Grave

Death comes slow
But determined.
Brother, son, father,
Destroyed
Justice, a distant memory.
Skin color determined worth.
Who would stand?
As the halos fall
He is carried away
Rights thin and frail
While the privileged laugh.
Color of hatred.
No man speaks,
Blood on their hands
Conspicuously,
They seek soap and water.

About the Author

Kathy M. Johnson is the author of My Bullying Handbook and is also a poet. She has been writing poetry for more than 50 years, having started at age seven. She enjoys reading, writing, and painting.

Kathy is the mother of two girls and a grandmother to four beautiful grandchildren, one boy, and three girls. She lives in Spokane, Washington, where she also grew up.

This poetry book is about life and death and the moments in between.

www.ingramcontent.com/pod-product-compliance
Lightning Source LLC
LaVergne TN
LVHW020937090426
835512LV00020B/3397